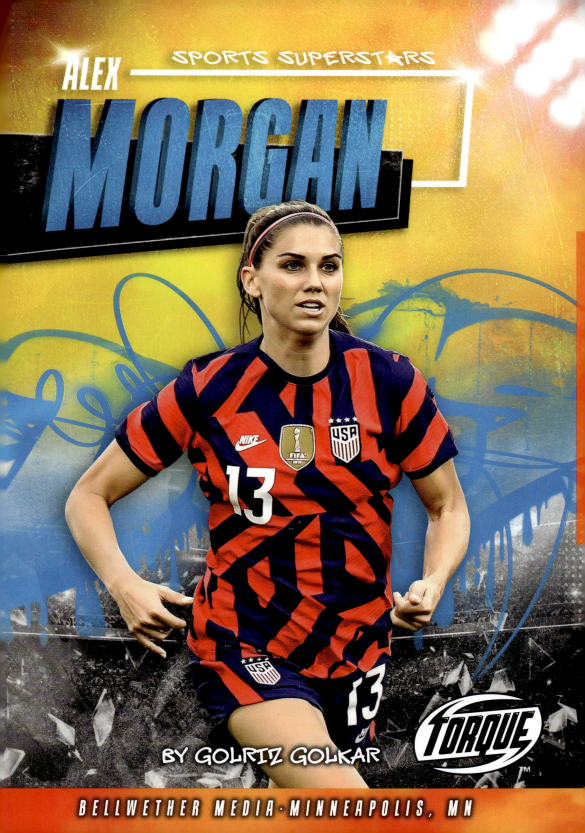

Torque brims with excitement perfect for thrill-seekers of all kinds. Discover daring survival skills, explore uncharted worlds, and marvel at mighty engines and extreme sports. In *Torque* books, anything can happen. Are you ready?

This edition first published in 2024 by Bellwether Media, Inc.

No part of this publication may be reproduced in whole or in part without written permission of the publisher. For information regarding permission, write to Bellwether Media, Inc., Attention: Permissions Department, 6012 Blue Circle Drive, Minnetonka, MN 55343.

Library of Congress Cataloging-in-Publication Data

Names: Golkar, Golriz, author.
Title: Alex Morgan / by Golriz Golkar.
Description: Minneapolis, MN : Bellwether Media, 2024. | Series: Sports superstars | Includes bibliographical references and index. | Audience: Ages 7-12 | Audience: Grades 4-6 | Summary: "Engaging images accompany information about Alex Morgan. The combination of high-interest subject matter and light text is intended for students in grades 3 through 7"– Provided by publisher.
Identifiers: LCCN 2023006483 (print) | LCCN 2023006484 (ebook) | ISBN 9798886874617 (library binding) | ISBN 9798886876499 (ebook)
Subjects: LCSH: Morgan, Alex (Alexandra Patricia), 1989–Juvenile literature. | Women soccer players–United States–Biography–Juvenile literature.
Classification: LCC GV942.7.M673 G65 2024 (print) | LCC GV942.7.M673 (ebook) | DDC 796.334092 [B]–dc23/eng/20230213
LC record available at https://lccn.loc.gov/2023006483
LC ebook record available at https://lccn.loc.gov/2023006484

Text copyright © 2024 by Bellwether Media, Inc. TORQUE and associated logos are trademarks and/or registered trademarks of Bellwether Media, Inc.

Editor: Rachael Barnes   Designer: Gabriel Hilger

Printed in the United States of America, North Mankato, MN.

TABLE OF CONTENTS

CHASING THE CHAMPIONSHIP.............. 4
WHO IS ALEX MORGAN? 6
A YOUNG SOCCER STAR................... 8
SOCCER SUPERSTAR 12
MORGAN'S FUTURE 20
GLOSSARY 22
TO LEARN MORE 23
INDEX 24

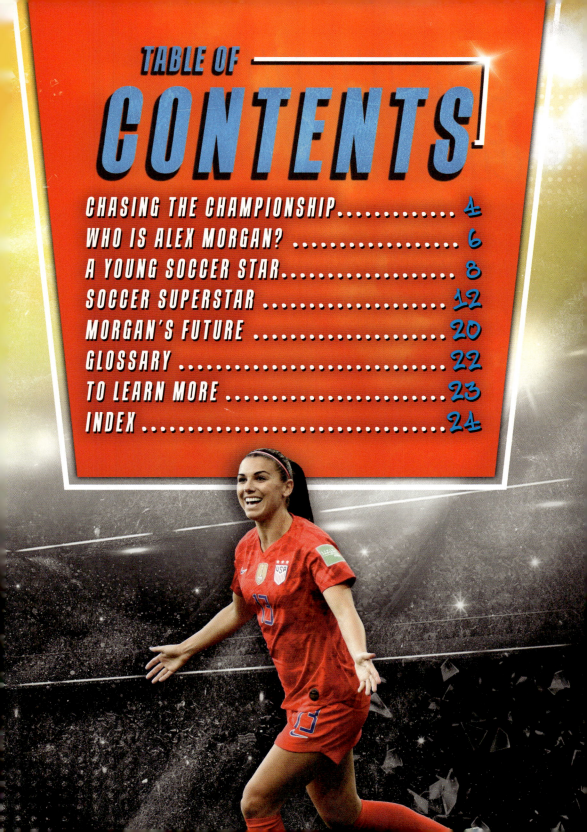

CHASING THE CHAMPIONSHIP

The United States is playing in the 2011 Women's **World Cup**. It is the **semifinal** and the team is leading 2–1 over France.

Alex Morgan controls the ball with four of France's players just behind her. She kicks the ball into the net. **Goal**! The U.S. team goes on to win the game.

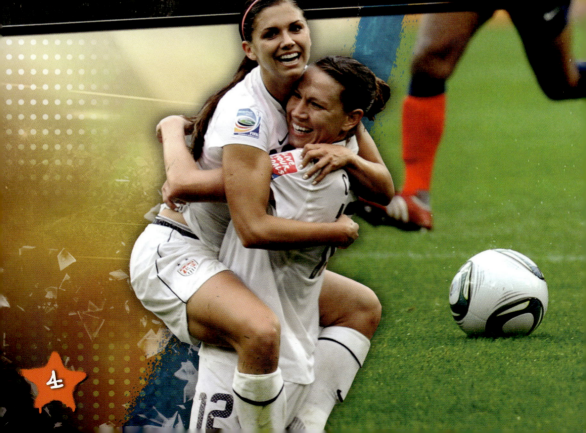

Top Scorer
Morgan has scored more than 100 goals in international soccer games.

WHO IS ALEX MORGAN?

Alex Morgan is a **professional** soccer player. She plays **forward**. She is a leading scorer on the U.S. Women's National Team (USWNT). Her speed and skills have led the team to **international** success.

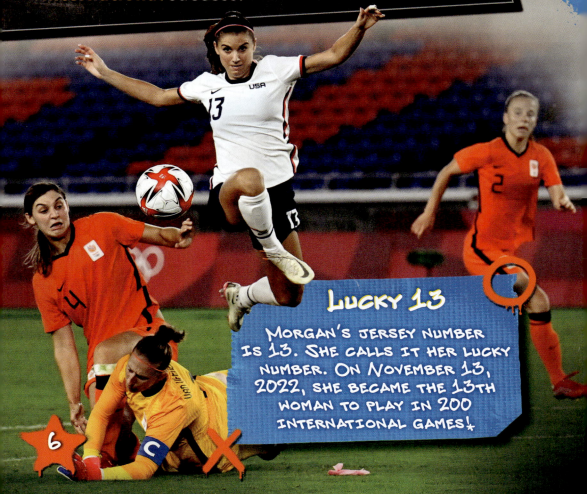

Lucky 13

Morgan's jersey number is 13. She calls it her lucky number. On November 13, 2022, she became the 13th woman to play in 200 international games!

ALEX MORGAN

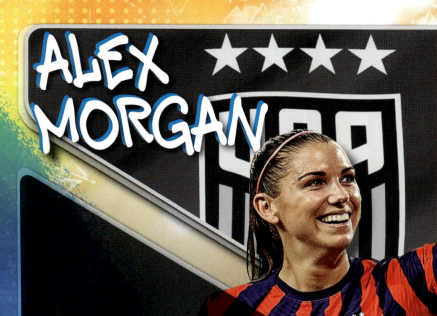

BIRTHDAY July 2, 1989

HOMETOWN Diamond Bar, California

POSITION forward

HEIGHT 5 feet 7 inches

DRAFTED Western New York Flash in the 1st round (1st overall) of the 2011 WPS draft

Morgan is also a businesswoman. Much of her work is about fighting for women's **equality**.

A YOUNG SOCCER STAR

Morgan played many sports as a child. At age 14, she decided to focus on soccer. She showed talent on her first soccer team.

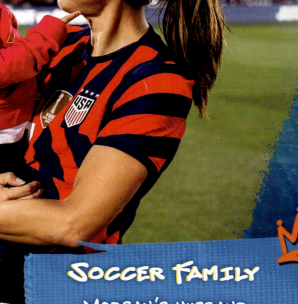

Soccer Family

Morgan's husband, Servando Carrasco, is also a professional soccer player. They have a daughter named Charlie.

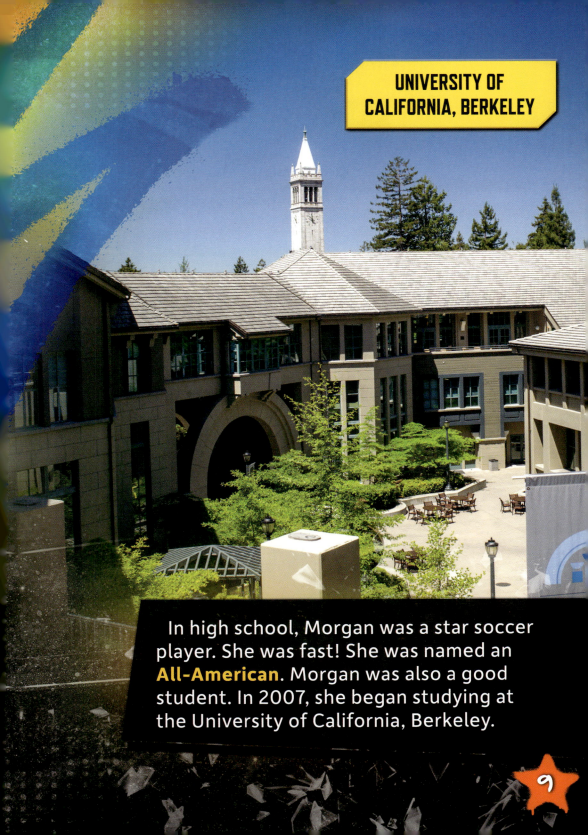

UNIVERSITY OF CALIFORNIA, BERKELEY

In high school, Morgan was a star soccer player. She was fast! She was named an **All-American**. Morgan was also a good student. In 2007, she began studying at the University of California, Berkeley.

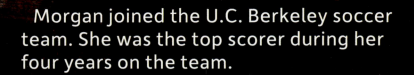

Morgan joined the U.C. Berkeley soccer team. She was the top scorer during her four years on the team.

In 2008, she played in the Under-20 Women's World Cup. She scored the goal that won the **championship**! In 2010, she graduated from U.C. Berkeley as a top student and soccer star.

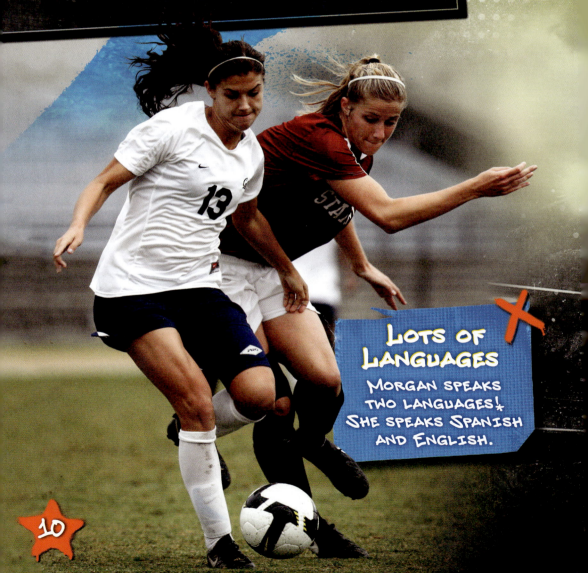

Lots of Languages

Morgan speaks two languages! She speaks Spanish and English.

FAVORITES

SHOES
Nike Dunks

FOOD
tacos

MOVIE
Catch Me If You Can

2008 UNDER-20 WOMEN'S WORLD CUP

SOCCER SUPERSTAR

After college, professional soccer teams hoped to sign Morgan. In 2011, Morgan was **drafted** by the Western New York Flash. She was the first pick of the draft!

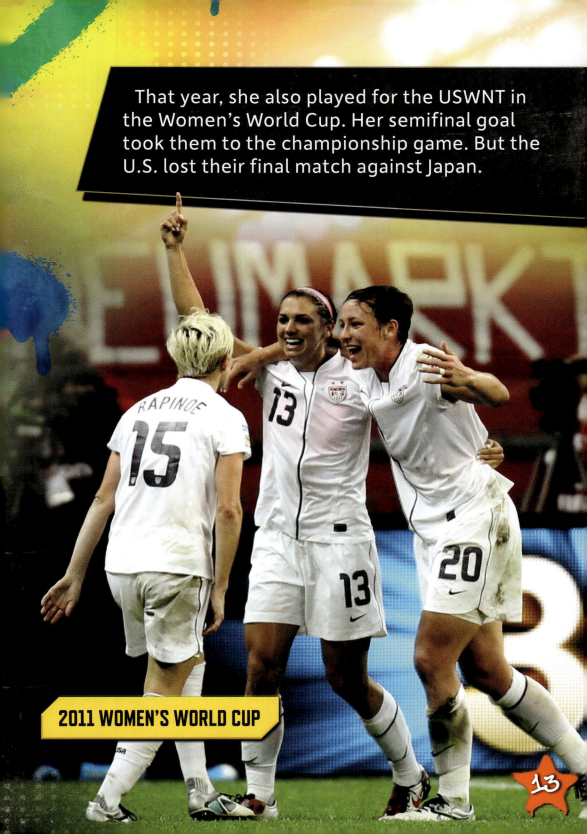

That year, she also played for the USWNT in the Women's World Cup. Her semifinal goal took them to the championship game. But the U.S. lost their final match against Japan.

2011 WOMEN'S WORLD CUP

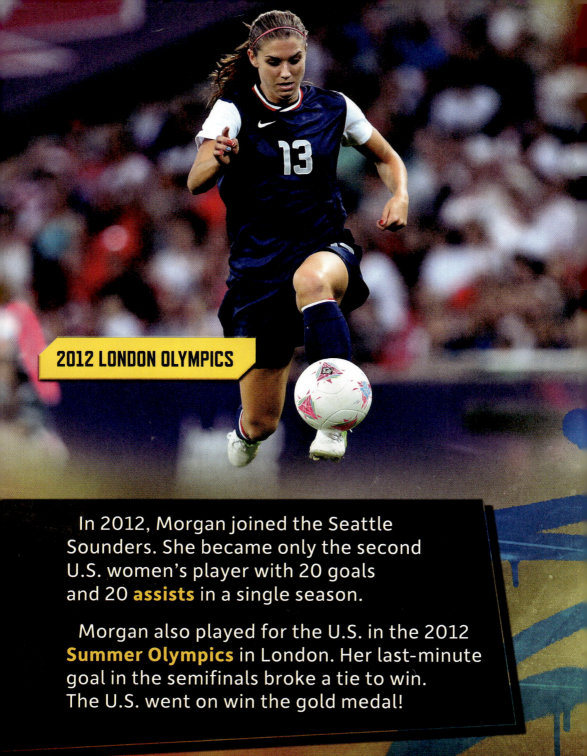

2012 LONDON OLYMPICS

In 2012, Morgan joined the Seattle Sounders. She became only the second U.S. women's player with 20 goals and 20 **assists** in a single season.

Morgan also played for the U.S. in the 2012 **Summer Olympics** in London. Her last-minute goal in the semifinals broke a tie to win. The U.S. went on win the gold medal!

ALEX MORGAN MAP

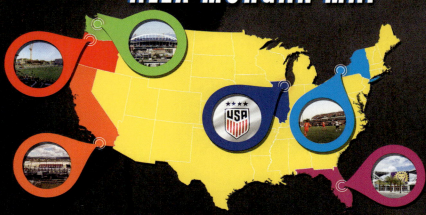

Western New York Flash, Elma, New York	2011
Seattle Sounders, Seattle, Washington	2012
Portland Thorns FC, Portland, Oregon	2013 to 2015
Orlando Pride, Orlando, Florida	2016 to 2021
San Diego Wave, San Diego, California	2021 to present
U.S. Women's National Team, Chicago, Illinois	2011 to present

2012 OLYMPIC GOLD MEDAL

In 2013, Morgan joined the Portland Thorns. In 2015, she played in her second Women's World Cup. But Morgan hurt her knee. It kept her out of the early games. Morgan still helped her team win the championship!

In 2016, she joined the Orlando Pride. She also played on the 2016 U.S. Olympic team in Rio de Janeiro. They won three games before losing to Sweden.

MORGAN PLAYING FOR THE PORTLAND THORNS

2015 WOMEN'S WORLD CUP

TROPHY SHELF

2 Olympic medals

2 FIFA Women's World Cup championships

2 U.S. Soccer Female Player of the Year awards

NWSL Golden Boot winner

4 CONCACAF Player of the Year awards

Morgan played in her third World Cup in 2019. She helped the U.S. win the championship! In 2021, she played in the Tokyo Olympics. The U.S. won the bronze medal.

Morgan has faced challenges. She and her USWNT teammates were not being paid the same as male players. They fought for equal pay. After a long legal battle, they won!

2019 WOMEN'S WORLD CUP

TIMELINE

— 2011 —
Morgan is drafted by the Flash

— 2012 —
Morgan signs with the Sounders

— 2013 —
Morgan joins the Thorns

Morgan wins an Olympic gold medal

MORGAN TALKING ABOUT EQUAL PAY

— 2015 —
Morgan wins her first Women's World Cup

— 2016 —
Morgan joins the Pride

— 2021 —
Morgan signs with the Wave

Morgan wins an Olympic bronze medal

MORGAN'S FUTURE

In 2021, Morgan and three other female **athletes** started Togethxr. The company shares stories about women in sports. They **inspire** young athletes.

Today, Morgan is a powerhouse player for the San Diego Wave. She continues to play for the USWNT, too. Morgan shines on and off the soccer field!

GLOSSARY

All-American—a title given to outstanding young athletes in different sports

assists—passes made from one soccer player to another who immediately scores

athletes—people who are trained in or good at games that require physical strength and skill

championship—a contest to decide the best team or person

drafted—selected by a professional team to play for them

equality—the state of being the same from one person to another

forward—a position in soccer that involves trying to score or help teammates score goals

goal—a point in soccer

inspire—to give someone an idea about what to do or create

international—involving two or more countries

professional—related to a player or team that makes money playing a sport

semifinal—a game played to decide who goes to the championship game

Summer Olympics—a worldwide summer sports contest held in a different country every four years

World Cup—an international soccer competition held every four years

TO LEARN MORE

AT THE LIBRARY

Abdo, Kenny. *Alex Morgan*. Minneapolis, Minn.: ABDO Zoom, 2021.

Bolte, Mari. *FIFA*. North Mankato, Minn.: Norwood House Press, 2023.

Chandler, Matt. *Alex Morgan: Soccer Champion*. North Mankato, Minn.: Capstone Press, 2020.

ON THE WEB

Factsurfer.com gives you a safe, fun way to find more information.

1. Go to www.factsurfer.com

2. Enter "Alex Morgan" into the search box and click 🔍.

3. Select your book cover to see a list of related content.

INDEX

All-American, 9
assists, 14
awards, 9, 14, 15, 17, 18
championship, 10, 13, 16, 18
childhood, 8, 9
draft, 12
equality, 7, 18, 19
family, 8
favorites, 11
forward, 6
goal, 4, 5, 10, 13, 14
hurt, 16
languages, 10
map, 15
number, 6
Orlando Pride, 16
Portland Thorns, 16
profile, 7
San Diego Wave, 21
Seattle Sounders, 14
Summer Olympics, 14, 15, 16, 18
timeline, 18–19
Togethxr, 20
trophy shelf, 17
Under-20 Women's World Cup, 10, 11
University of California, Berkeley, 9, 10
U.S. Women's National Team, 4, 6, 13, 14, 16, 18, 21
Western New York Flash, 12
Women's World Cup, 4, 13, 16, 17, 18

The images in this book are reproduced through the courtesy of: Dustin Bradford/ Icon Sportswire/ AP Images, front cover; feelphoto, p. 3; Martin Meissner/ AP Images, pp. 4, 4-5; Xinhua/ Alamy, pp. 6-7; Robin Alam/ Icon Sportswire/ AP Images, p. 7; United States Soccer Federation, pp. 7 (USWNT logo), 15 (USWNT logo); Brad Smith/ ISI Photos/ Contributor/ Getty Images, p. 8; gary yim, p. 9; San Francisco Chronicle/ Hearst Newspapers via Getty Images/ Contributor/ Getty Images, p. 10; Santiago Llanquin/ AP Images, p. 11; Christophe Decaix, p. 11 (Nike Dunks); Pixel-Shot, p. 11 (tacos); BFA/ Alamy, p. 11 (*Catch Me If You Can*); Mike Zarrilli/ Contributor/ Getty Images, p. 12; Michael Probst/ AP Images, p. 13; Mo Khursheed/ AP Images, pp. 14, 15 (2012 gold medal); Zuma Press, Inc./ AP Images, p. 15 (New York); Ian Dewar Photography, p. 15 (Seattle); Yooran Park, p. 15 (Portland); Matthew Kaiser 7, p. 15 (Orlando); Durson Services Inc., p. 15 (San Diego); David Blair/ AP Images, pp. 16-17; Rich Lam/ Stringer/ Getty Images, p. 17; SOPA Images Limited/ Alamy, p. 18 (2019 Women's World Cup); Tony Baggett, p. 18 (2012); Manuel Balce Ceneta/ AP Images, pp. 18-19; Romain Biard, pp. 19 (Women's World Cup trophy), 23; fifg, p. 19 (2021); Cal Sport Media/ Alamy, p. 20; Azael Rodriguez/ Stringer/ Getty Images, pp. 20-21.

24